the Towers of Numar

by Michel Gagné

For Josie, who's always doing nice things for people.

GAGNÉ
International
Press

ISBN 0-9719053-3-9

For information please write to:
GAGNÉ International Press
1225 E. Sunset Drive, Ste 145 PMB 336
Bellingham, WA 98226-3554
gagneint@aol.com
www.gagneint.com

Printed in Canada

10 9 8 7 6 5 4 3 2 1

First Edition

The world of Numar was a beautiful place
where lived a kind and civilized race.

Crazy as it may sound,
Numerions were anchored to the ground.

The funny thing is,
they could still move with ease,
fleeing and flowing around
as they pleased.

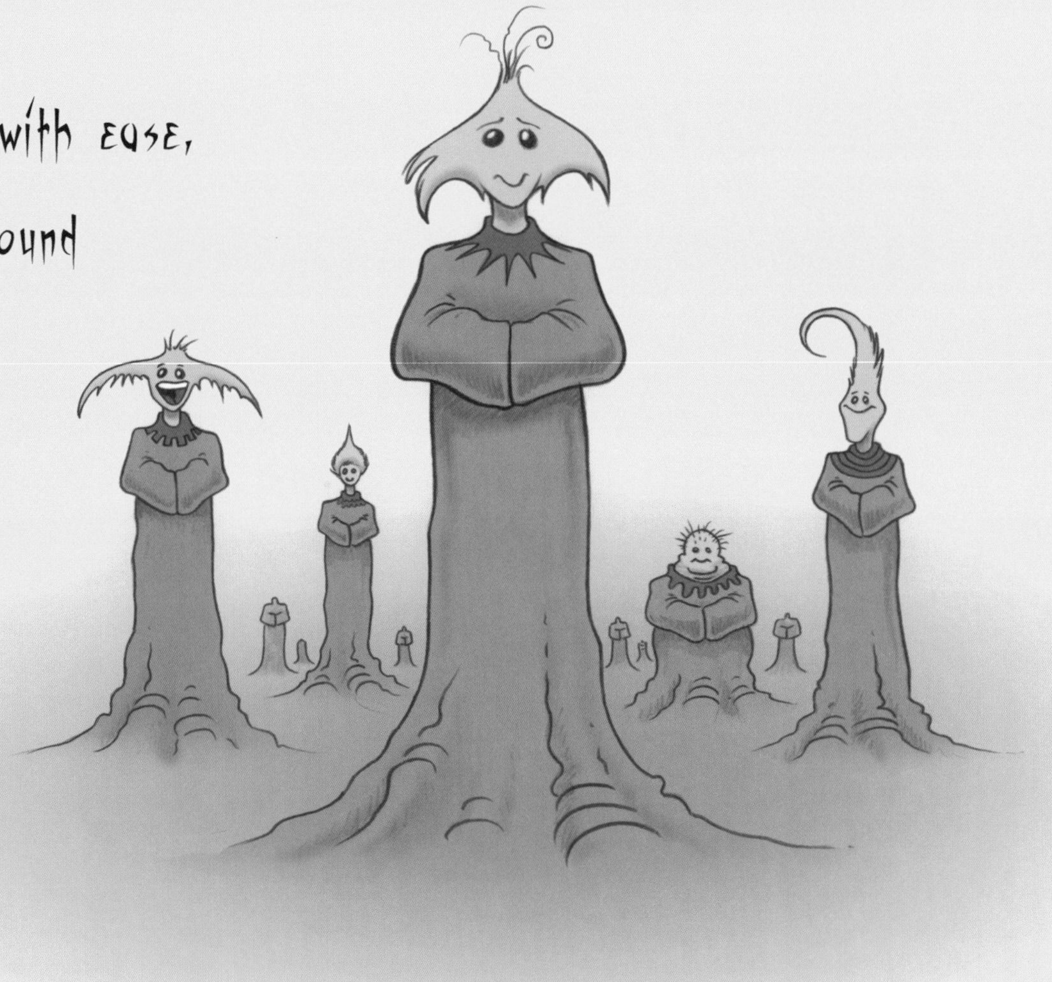

Now let's begin our story, shall we?

On the first day of a new century,
Meeka was born, a healthy baby.

Meeka grew up in the small town of Plience,

where she developed aptitudes

for art and science.

One could say
without fear of exageration,
that she demonstrated
great imagination.

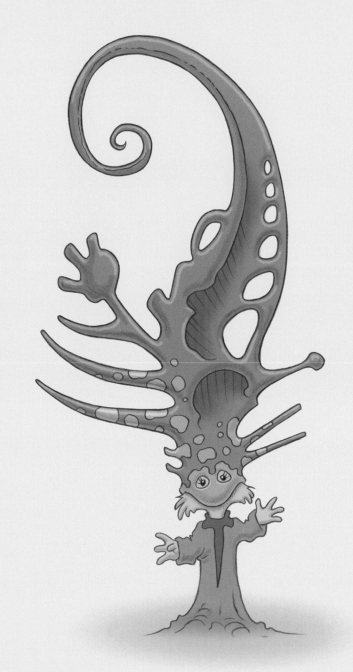

Her smiling sculptures

made everyone happy,

they even filled Grumpy Goomo with glee.

Her fascination for transportation,

gave birth to a radical invention.

Before long, she had total fame,

every Numarian knew her name.

By the tender age of eighteen, she was a renowned architect, who was commissioned to design the sacred shrine of Hishtek.

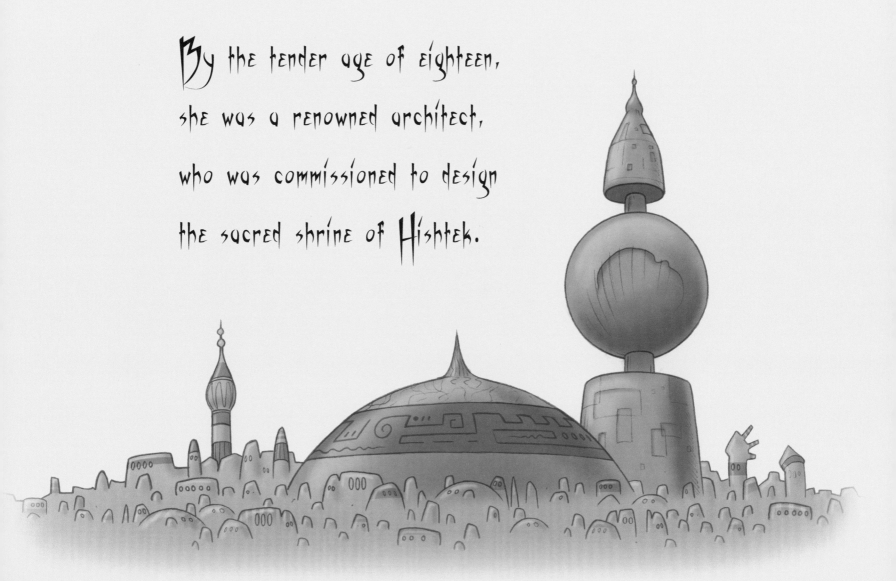

She was barely twenty,
when she started to play
with anti-gravity.

Pretty incredible,
wouldn't you say?

Meeka had become

Numar's greatest achiever,

surpassing herself

with each new endeavor.

Still, no one was expecting

her next big thing...

With a cash investment
and an army of workers,
Meeka started to build
the tallest of all towers.

The gigantic structure grew,
and grew, and grew.
How far would it go?
No one really knew.

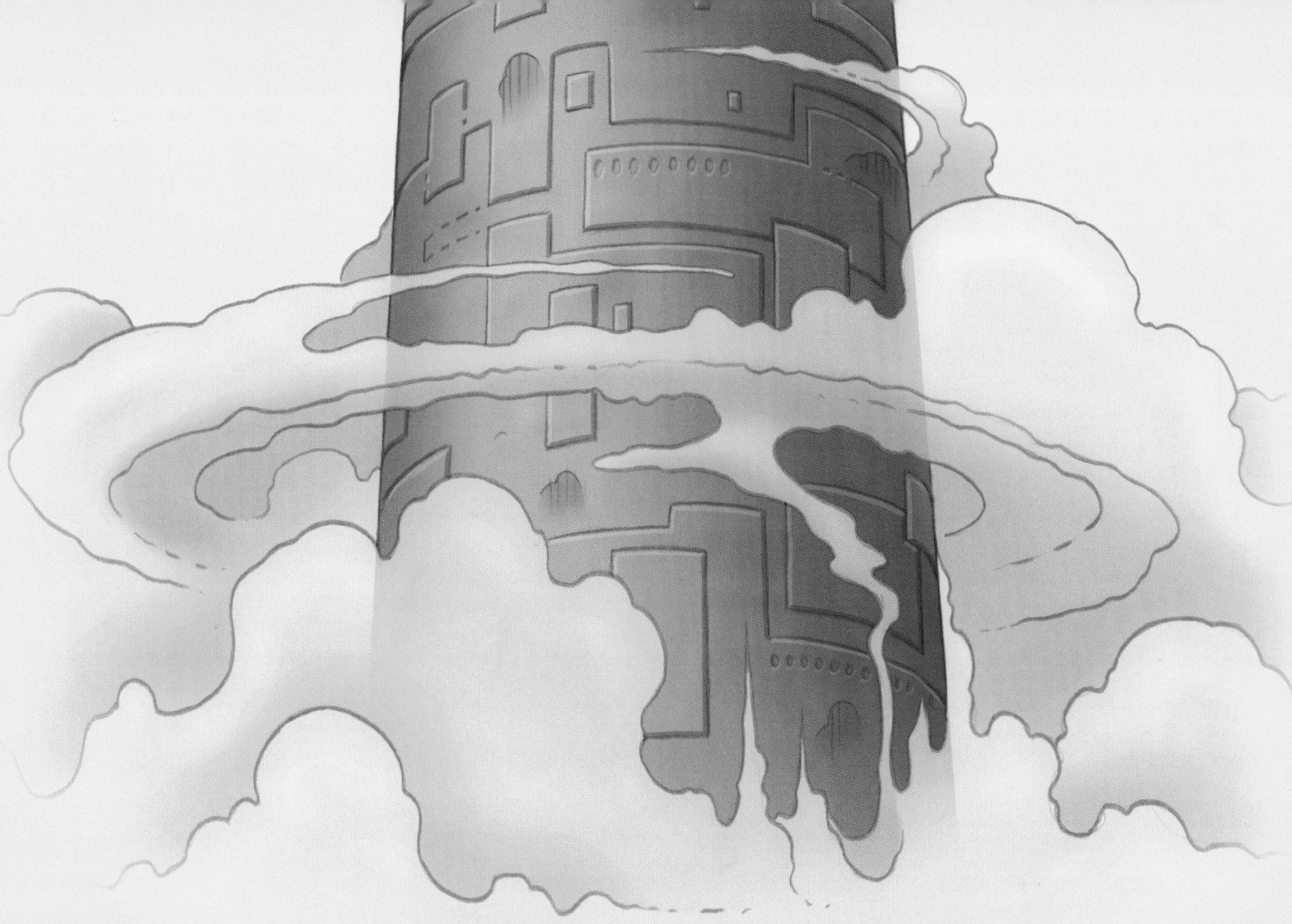

It grew over the clouds,

past the atmosphere,

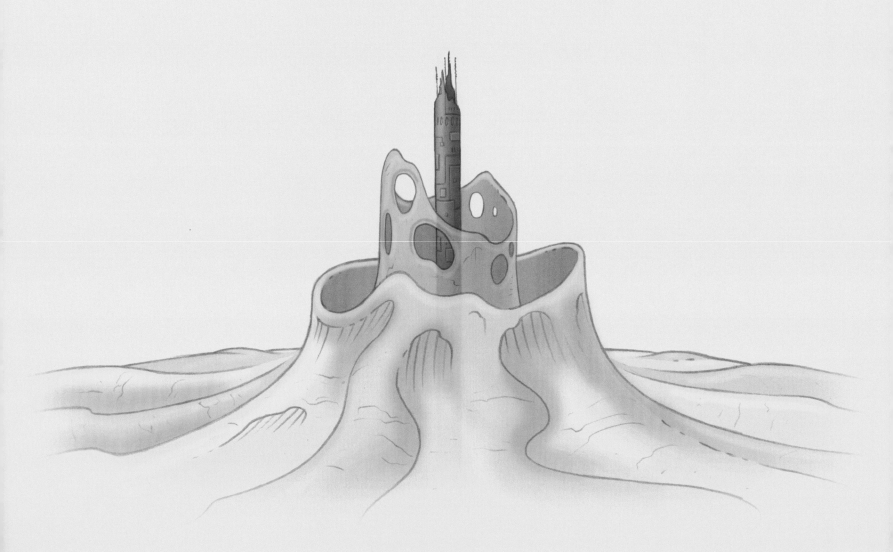

higher and higher,   like a giant spear.

It hit its peak
as it touched the ground.

And so it was, that a new world was found.

The Numerians were ecstatic!

They were amazed!

They rewarded Meeko with medals and praise.

Triumphant yet exhausted, Meeka retreated.
She went to the gardens of Neece,
where she meditated in peace.

Rejuvenated and full of joy,

she peeked through her observational toy.

What she saw with that telescope,
made Meeka think on a much higher scope.

With great patience and a lot of hard work,
she designed what she called a "Cosmic Network".

More towers were erected, growing tall until connected.
Numerian life spread into space. A new era was taking place.

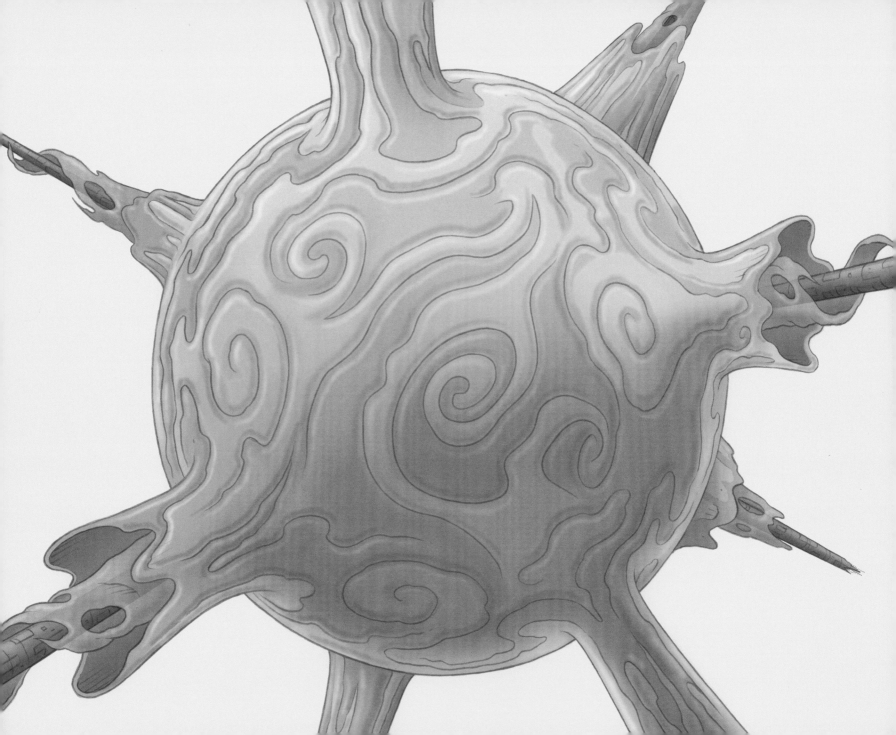

What started as

something really cool,

just happened to be the prime molecule,

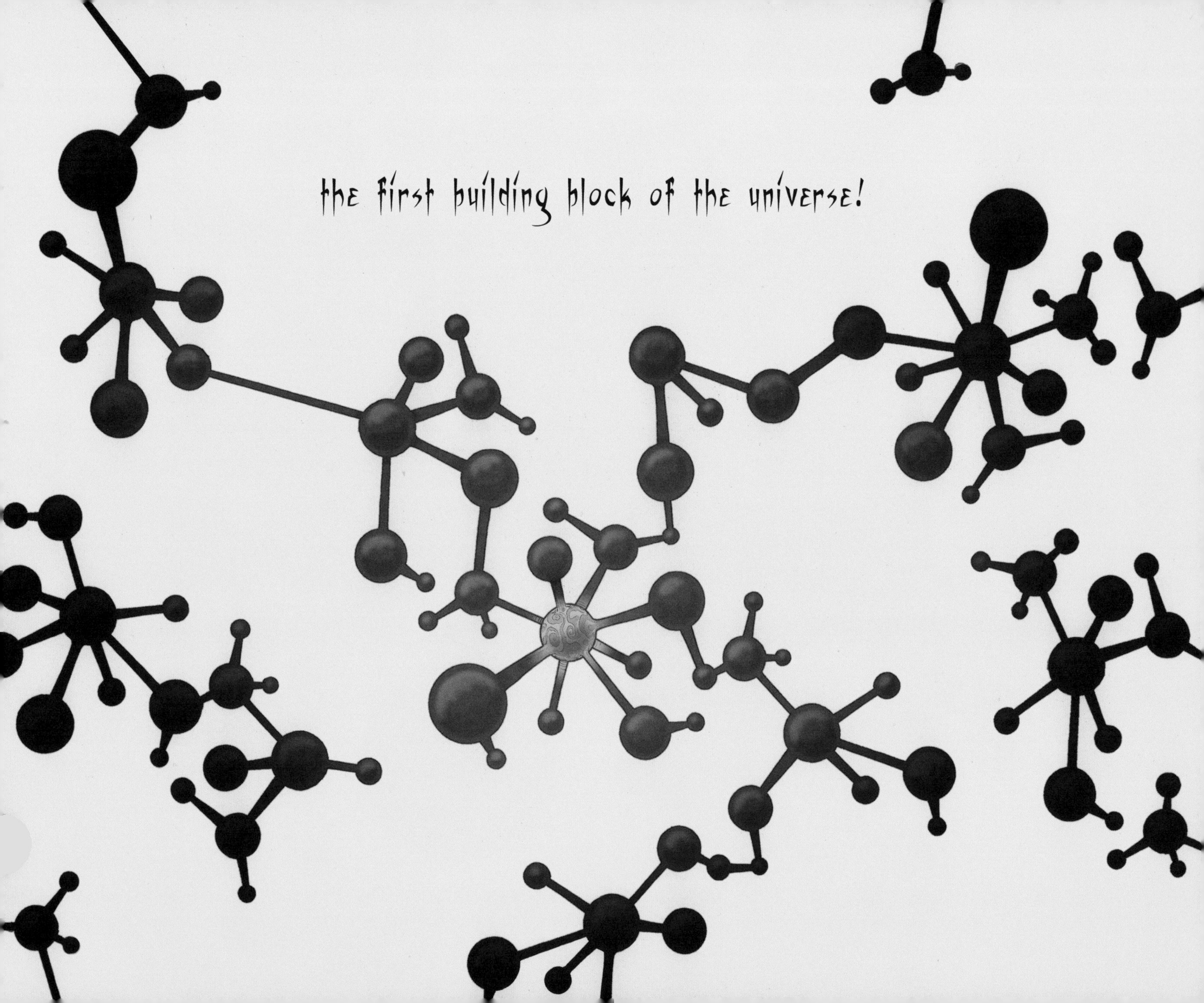
the first building block of the universe!

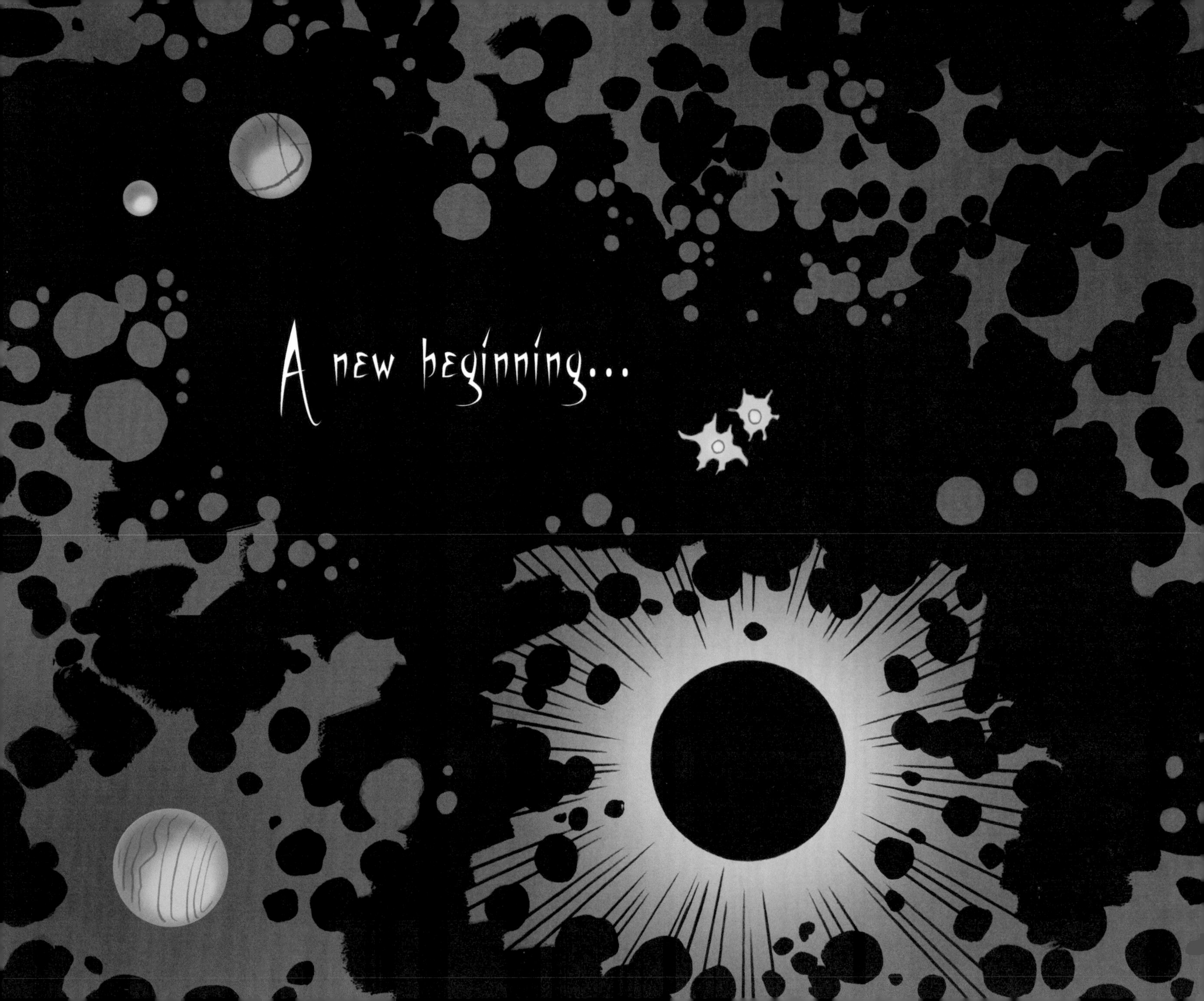
A new beginning...

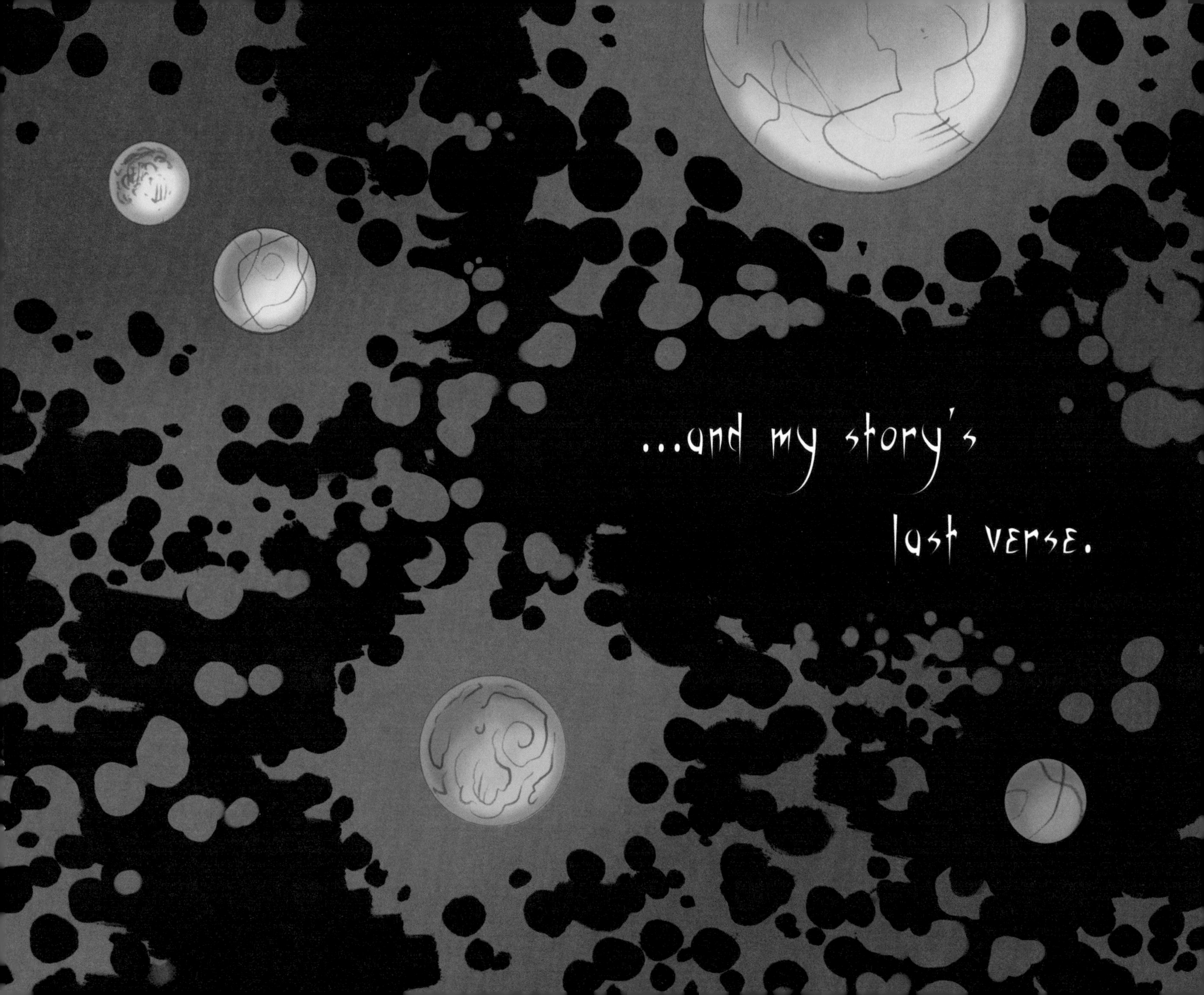
...and my story's
last verse.

MICHEL GAGNÉ

Michel Gagné was born in Québec, Canada. As a young man, he studied animation at Sheridan College School of Visual Arts in Ontario, Canada.

In 1985, he began a highly successful career drawing characters and special effects for animated and live-action feature films. Gagné's work has appeared in films such as "The Iron Giant", "Osmosis Jones", "The Land Before Time", "All Dogs Go to Heaven", "An American Tail", and numerous others. His 3 ½ minute independent short film, "Prelude to Eden", is a favorite among animation students and teachers, and has played in festivals throughout the world. Michel was honored by the International Animated Film Society, ASIFA-Hollywood, with four Annie Award nominations. He continues to design and consult on major film projects.

The creator made the jump to print in 1998 with his critically acclaimed first book, "A Search for Meaning: The Story of Rex", and the birth of GAGNÉ International Press. Teaming up with his beloved wife Nancy, he continues to expand the Gagné library, solidifying his reputation as an alternative book publisher. In 2002, Michel was given carte blanche to write and illustrate a 40-page Batman story for DC Comics. His bizarre and highly controversial tale, "Spore", was serialized in "Detective Comics", issues #776-780.

Among his other creative endeavors, Michel has experimented in a variety of mediums including sculptures, paintings and mixed-medias. He lives peacefully with his wife and two dogs, in the Pacific Northwest.

This book uses the Vampiress font, designed by Nate Piekos.